THE ZIONIST

Why You Should Move To Israel

Ian Pear

The Zionist

Copyright © 2011 Ian Pear

Edited by David and Faranak Margolese

All rights reserved.

ISBN-10: 1463533276

ISBN-13: 978-1463533274

iandanielpear@gmail.com

CONTENTS

1 Why Judaism Has Failed   1

2 Why A State Matters   32

3 Why Land Matters   41

4 Ancient Israel   63

5 The State Of Israel   86

6 Imagine   91

7 The Zionist   99

1 WHY JUDAISM HAS FAILED

In high school, I was a wrestler. Not a very good one, but a wrestler nonetheless. Before each match I, along with all the other wrestlers on both opposing teams, had to weigh in. One time, I remember standing across from a particularly mean looking opponent. His coach called him up to the scale with a booming voice: "In the 171 pound weight class ... from Washington High School," *and then a slight pause,* "CHAINSAW!"

Up to the scale walked a massively built man. As I recall, he was one solid muscle; had a tattoo that began at his toe and wound up his body all the way to his neck; and most threatening of all, he had a menacing, Neanderthal-looking unibrow that stretched across his forehead. I was intimidated.

I turned to my coach. I knew I was going to lose to this guy; how could I not? But I didn't need to let my opponent know that now. I didn't need to give him an edge and reveal just how terrified and totally intimidated I was. And thus, it was with a great sigh of relief when I saw my coach wink at me. He would not allow Chainsaw the edge in intimidation. He would give me a good, equally fierce nickname, one that would no doubt strike fear in the heart of Chainsaw just like his name had done to me.

What name would my coach give me, I wondered. *Would it be Faceripper? Or maybe The Mutilator?* And then he began, in a voice even more powerful than the voice of my challenger's coach: "From Sunnyslope High School…at 171 pounds," *I held my breath, wondering what the name would be? Raging warrior? The Destroyer?*

And then, with a slight smile forming at the corners of his lips, he bellowed: "THE MATZA BALL!"

As you might imagine, I did not enter the match with the intimidation factor on my side.

After the match – which is to say after I regained consciousness – I asked my coach why in the world he gave me such a name. His response was crushing, not because it assured my defeat, but rather for what it said about Judaism. His reasoning was as follows: Yes, he had wanted to make a joke of sorts, but he also wanted to root it in something plausible. So he decided he would identify me by giving me a nickname in the same general way I would identify myself. And when he thought of how I might choose to identify myself, he thought – and was right to think so – *Jewish*.

Consequently, when my coach told me that he decided to identify me as a Jew, I was not upset at all, nor did I question even for a moment that his comment might have been anti-Semitic. Not only was he a wonderful friend of the Jewish community, but *he was also right*. Being Jewish is exactly how I would have identified myself – and proudly so.

What did crush me, though, was the *means* by which he chose to identify me as a Jew. Rather than relating to thousands of years of inspiring history, essential contributions in the fields of morality, science, and philosophy, or at least alluding to one of the strong men of Jewish history such as King David or Samson, he named me after a mere cultural phenomenon – one of our gastronomical contributions to American society.

When I challenged him on this matter, he replied: "But that's all I know about Judaism."

Why Has Judaism Failed?

Never before had I heard such a powerful and convincing indictment against the efficacy of Judaism in America. Here was a friend, a decent and kind non-Jew, whose ignorance was honest and without malicious intent, but brutal nevertheless. If this man – a person who would have gladly given credit to the Jews for Judaism's contributions to the world if he had known of them – did not see anything more meaningful about Judaism than a matza ball, then what of the rest of the country? What about the rest of the world? Obviously, we must assume they too lack a deep appreciation, or for that matter *any* appreciation for what Judaism is supposed to be all about.

And that, to my great dismay, means that Judaism, despite its many great accomplishments worldwide, must ultimately be considered an international failure. After all, Judaism's *raison d'etre* is to spread its message of ethical monotheism to the rest of the world and inspire action to fight evil, eliminate poverty and hunger and protect the innocent.

If the rest of the world has no understanding about Judaism's *idea*, if the very population Judaism targets to receive its ethical monotheism message is oblivious to it, then it is obvious that Jews have not succeeded in fulfilling their mission. This is not to say that Jews have not accomplished anything of great import; of course we have. Jewish contributions in a whole host of fields are renowned. It is to say, however, that unfortunately the main contribution – the contribution envisioned by Judaism as its *sine qua non,* the reason for its very existence – *that contribution* has not been sufficiently made.

And thus, according to its own definition, Judaism has failed.

The question is why? Why has Judaism failed? Surely the message of ethical monotheism and its moral implications is a convincing argument and necessary value for world improvement. So why has it not infiltrated the four corners of the world?

A Light Unto The Nations

Let us begin to answer this question by examining just what it means to be "a light unto the nations." Just how are we supposed to accomplish this? We are so tiny in number, that even if every Jew were an ethical hero, we would still lack the strength, influence and global reach to fully confront the various challenges plaguing the world. In absolute terms, Jews are simply too inconsequential to fight evil, eliminate poverty and hunger and protect the innocent on a worldwide basis.

But Judaism never envisioned that we would have to. Rather, the job of the Jewish people is to spread the message of ethical monotheism to the nations of the world who are numerous enough to fight evil and poverty and hunger on a global scale. Jews need not create the infrastructure, possess the material strengths nor invent the intellectual know-how to solve all these problems; rather, we simply need to channel

– through inspiration – the already existing assets of others in the right direction.

Maybe this relationship is what was intended by God's challenge to the Jewish people, quoted in the Book of the Prophet Isaiah, to be "a light unto the nations." The Jewish people need not accomplish everything by themselves – and indeed, they would not be able to even if they so desired. Instead they must provide the *light* necessary to do so. With this example, these same nations will then be prepared to fight against – and have the ability to eliminate – evil in the world.

This understanding lends itself well to the phrase which appears in Isaiah: "I, God, will *give* you, the Jewish people, to the nations of the world to serve as a light unto the nations, *so that* My salvation may reach the ends of the earth." Consider the two important points highlighted by the italicized words. First, the Jewish people are given by God to others; the purpose of Jewish existence is service to others - not for our own benefit. Second, notice that the ultimate goal God envisions is that the entire world – literally the ends of the earth – will be reached by His salvation. *This goal can only be reached when the Jews provide the light to other nations who can actually fulfill it.*

Our job, therefore, is to inspire friends and fair minded people to enter the battle, to defend morality and fight against those indifferent to – and often in opposition to – God's vision of a more compassionate, enlightened and holy world. As the number of these nations grow, as it has for millennia now, so too does the impact Judaism will have on the international stage.

Jewish Communities

Even if every Jew were a saint, and even if every waking hour of every one of these saints' lives were spent unselfishly dedicated to improving the lives of others, the Jewish people would still not be able to positively touch the lives of every human on the planet. There simply are too many people in need and too few Jews capable of offering necessary aid.

It is for this reason that many of those Jews most concerned with improving the world join organized Jewish communities. Their hope is to amplify their efforts through the added effectiveness and reach offered by a strong community, perhaps a UJA, a hospital, or a synagogue food bank.

But the problem is that communities, too, are not sufficient. Just as individual Jews are limited in their ability to impact the entire world, so too are individual communities. For example, let's suppose that the UJA Federation of Boston has a highly effective food distribution program that aids needy Jewish people in the Boston area. That's great, but what about the rest of the country? How does the UJA benefit the non-Jewish population of Idaho? And for that matter, how does it get food to the starving people in

Uganda and Rwanda? How wide an influence can one individual – or even an entire Jewish community – have in these places? And even if a community decides to spend all of its efforts and limited resources on changing the situation in these places, what about the rest of the world? What about Thailand, Peru or India? The UJA Federation of Boston, no matter how effective, cannot be everywhere.

Yet, the mission given to the Jewish people *is* to be everywhere – to liberate the enslaved everywhere, uplift the oppressed *everywhere* and give hope to the shattered *everywhere*. Therefore, such limited efforts – despite the good they achieve must be considered ultimately inadequate.

The Jewish Nation

Returning to our question as to why Judaism has failed, the answer is that the Jewish people cannot truly fulfill its mission – and cannot fully be a light unto the nations – *without first becoming a nation itself.*

While it is true, of course, that a Jewish nation also cannot be in all places at all times, just as an individual and community cannot, it does not have to be for its impact to be felt. Through modeling, its efforts can inspire other nations, which in turn *can* impact all the peoples of the Earth. Through modeling its activities to other nations, through acting in such an exemplary way that inspires other nations to act similarly, the

Jewish nation can reach everywhere even if it cannot physically be everywhere. It can do so because nations are influenced by, and emulate, other nations, and everyone lives within a nation.

Being a nation can be defined three ways. It can simply be a people united by things such as culture, language or religion, but who do not necessarily live in one particular area. Or it can mean a state with a sovereign government. Or it can be both; a people with a common heritage who live in their own state with a sovereign government – a *nation-state*.

When I refer to the need of the Jewish people to become a nation itself in order to be a light unto the nations, I mean with our own state and sovereign government. I mean a nation-state.

A nation of people dispersed and diluted throughout the world simply is not powerful enough to fulfill this global redeeming role. Similarly, a political state governed by Jews but devoid of common values and purpose is also not capable of successfully impacting the world in a dramatic fashion. No, for Jews to properly fulfill their role of spreading the message of ethical monotheism they must possess a nation-state based on our unique Jewish heritage, the most potent agent of international change.

Unfortunately, the last 2,000 years of exile have precluded this option for the Jewish people. As a consequence, outstanding as Jewish contributions to humanity during this period have been, they simply have not been world-transforming. The reestablishment of Israel in 1948 – which is the rebirth of the State of the Nation of Jewish people – thus represents a great transformation in the nature of the Jewish ability to redeem the world. With it, the Jewish impact on the world left the realm of individual contribution and entered the potential for national contribution.

This answers the question; if Judaism is so great, if its message is so powerful, why has it failed to fully breach the consciousness of the world? Why have the intended results not been achieved?

The answer is that Judaism has failed because, while the message and the messengers have been present, the *means* necessary to implement the message on a worldwide scale was not. The means necessary is the Jewish nation-state, which if taken advantage of properly has the potential to transform the world. Indeed, as we shall see, the last time Judaism made revolutionary contributions to the world on a global scale was over 2000 years ago when we last had sovereignty in the land of Israel.

The Power Of The Group

Imagine yourself grabbing a small twig off the branch of a tree. Now break it. Pretty easy, right? Now take ten twigs of equal width and quality and bind them together. Try to break the twigs. Not as easy? Perhaps even difficult? Maybe even impossible?

Just as ten twigs together are collectively much stronger than ten twigs independently, so too are ten people acting in unison more powerful – their efforts more effective, more enduring, and far reaching – than ten people acting as individuals. The whole of their actions are simply much greater than the sum of their parts.

On almost any given day and in almost any given aspect of life, we witness the truth that teamwork trumps personal endeavor in a variety of ways. Allow me to offer but one example of what I mean:

A number of years ago, when I was a graduate student in New York City, I designed a special program called "Practicing Random Acts of Kindness – The Date." The idea behind this initiative was simple. Rather than take a young woman out for an evening date in the traditional manner of dinner and a movie, I jotted down a list of potential acts of kindness we could do together and let her choose which one we should pursue. During the date, we hopefully accomplished something good for the world – at least in some small way. A hungry person was fed. A lonely person was comforted.

Imagine the impact if 100 individuals designed a similar dating experience. Now imagine if a different 100 individuals decided to work together as a team to undertake whatever charitable endeavor the first 100 people decided to pursue. If the charitable endeavor chosen by our hypothetical participants was to make sandwiches to distribute to the homeless population of New York City, which group – the 100 individuals or the team of 100 – do you think would accomplish more?

For a number of different reasons, the answer is the second group, the people working together.

For starters, the team of sandwich makers would be able to produce many more sandwiches and thus feed far more people, despite possessing the exact same resources as the group of 100 individuals. But the team could also pool their resources, and enjoy greater buying power than any one individual. If, for example, the ingredients for each sandwich cost $1 at a retail supermarket, the 100 individuals would each be forced to spend $1 per sandwich, thus altogether spending $100 to produce 100 sandwiches. But the group could take their $100 and buy the same ingredients wholesale for only $50. They could produce 200 sandwiches with the same amount of money.

Pooling resources also creates the opportunity to think big. Let's say a new sandwich-making machine has just been created – one that can produce astronomical amounts of perfectly formed and delicious sandwiches – and is now available for purchase for $25. Our sandwich-making endeavor would benefit tremendously by incorporating this machine into its efforts. The individual sandwich makers, of course, could never purchase such a contraption.

After all, they have but $1 available to each of them – and that $1 has to buy the ingredients necessary for the sandwich. The collective group of 100, however, has the luxury to consider the merits of purchasing the machine. Its efficiency would enable more people to be reached and free up their time to perform other meritorious acts.

Of course, a sandwich machine may not strike us as such a meaningful expenditure of limited resources. But what if the question at hand was whether to upgrade the infrastructure of a poor community to include phone services, fire trucks, or a sewage line? These items require a meaningful investment, which can only be achieved by pooling resources. Without reaching a critical mass, the community will have no fire truck at all. There is no halfway choice. Individuals working alone will never be able to consider these possibilities; groups can.

Pooling of resources, however, is not just about greater financial buying power. In fact, some of its greatest assets lie in the social fields. The group of 100 members will not just pool their money; they will also share their social networks, brainstorm ideas, and provide emotional support. Each of these benefits, in turn, will further increase the advantage of the group's accomplishments vis-à-vis the 100 individuals' efforts.

But the advantages don't end there. Thanks to the benefits of division of labor, the group can distribute its 200 sandwiches in less time than the 100 individuals. Those who are experts in making the sandwiches will make the sandwiches, while those better at distribution will take care of delivery, and so on. All of the individuals working apart, meanwhile, will have to complete the various facets of the whole job themselves – buying the ingredients, making the sandwiches, identifying worthy recipients, traveling to the beneficiaries, and providing follow up services. As a consequence, the individuals will likely accomplish much less – offering fewer sandwiches and less auxiliary benefits – while taking more time.

The division of labor may not seem so important in this limited case. After all, making a sandwich is not rocket science, so there might not be too significant a difference if an amateur takes this job as opposed to a seasoned professional. But what if the endeavor being undertaken *is* rocket science – or for that matter, any field requiring highly-qualified expertise? In such cases, the individuals would expend more time and resources and produce a lower quality product than the multi-talented group.

Finally, individual behavior is unreliable. For even when a person has the best of intentions, many other forces may intrude on his capacity to do good. Maybe he gets sick. Maybe he oversleeps. Maybe he has to move to a new town. In each of these cases, the man on the street he intends to help goes hungry.

In contrast, teams eliminate the vagaries of individual behavior. While each individual member of a group may have his own life, the group itself is singular in focus and has but one solitary purpose – the one defined by its charter. And thus, even when individual members within the group are pulled in a variety of directions, the group as a whole nevertheless moves forward. People oversleeping, moving away, or just plain giving up do not interrupt its services; no matter what, they are provided on a consistent basis.

Try With All Your Might

It is for all these reasons that when a person sets out to accomplish something of great importance, he most likely will seek out others to join him. If a person wants to run for a political office, he certainly does not try to do it alone. He joins a political party and inspires its members to embrace his mission and help him. He avails himself of the financial resources of others, sets up support networks in every state, involves tens of thousands of volunteers, hires the best staff, and leans on experienced advisors. In short, he attempts to create an entire movement with a massive campaign team.

The Chasidic Rabbis tell a beautiful story on this subject. A father and son were once walking in the forest when they happened upon a large boulder in their way. The father turned to the son and said that if he – the son – tried with all his might and all his strength he surely would be able to move the enormous stone. The boy was skeptical, but since his father promised him, he tried nevertheless. He pushed, he pulled, he pounded, all to no avail. His father, however, continued to encourage him. "If you try with all your strength, you will be able to move the rock." The son tried again and again, but still without success. Finally, he turned to his father and said "You lied to me. You said if I tried with all my strength I would be able to move the rock ... but I cannot."

"No, my son" the father retorted. "You didn't use all your strength. You didn't ask me for help."

Teams working together simply do better and accomplish more than individuals working independently, no matter how talented such independent individuals may be. As such, if one wishes to accomplish matters of great meaning and great difficulty, one must join others – or inspire others to join him. An individual's strength is ultimately determined by the collective strength of those around him on whom he can rely.

2 WHY A STATE MATTERS

When A Nation Is Also A State

When it comes to Judaism and it's far reaching lofty goals, teamwork is not just beneficial, it is absolutely essential. And the teams that matter most on the international stage are of course, nations. Or more specifically, sovereign *nation-states*.

As mentioned earlier, a nation can be defined as a community of people who are bound together by a common culture, language or belief system. But a state is the *political* mechanism by which a nation fulfills its national values and vision.

Why A State Matters

A state influences its own population through the creation of laws and their enforcement, the establishment of services to provide social benefits, and allocating financial resources to pursue wider political goals. But it also has the potential – if it so chooses – to influence the broader populations of the world through military, diplomatic, economic, and humanitarian actions. To accomplish these goals, states must possess a population, a territory, and a sovereign government.

When a nation is also a state, it becomes an incredibly powerful and effective communal unit. The state is like a car, enabling the population or "driver" to get to where he wants to go. Just as the driver determines where his car goes, the nation determines the direction it wants its state to take. And just as the car provides the horsepower to get the driver to his destination, so too the state provides the political power to propel the nation on whatever journey it chooses to embark upon.

Obviously, many other sources of power exist that possess positive and essential qualities to move the world towards a utopian goal – from agencies such as the United Way, the Salvation Army and the Red Cross, to organizations like the United Nations or the World Court. However, none of these entities enjoy the same degree of power, direct access to and control over people, and allegiance as nation-states do. Nation-states operate on a level wholly above that of any other organization, community or mass movement.

Take, for instance, the tragedy of the Indian Ocean Tsunami in 2004. Immediately following the horrific event, scores of aid agencies jumped to action – except that they couldn't actually jump in until a nation-state became involved as well. For example, many of the survivors in most desperate need could not be reached except by helicopter, delivered via aircraft carrier and accompanied by armed escorts. Obviously, most aid agencies lacked the resources to purchase such equipment, especially given the fact that such agencies are dependent on the whims of public charitable support. Only nation-states – with their power to tax and thus legally enforce the pooling of necessary resources – possess this ability.

Just as important, even when the aid agencies were physically able to reach the survivors, they were not legally permitted to do so without permission granted from the host nations. Without the acquiescence of nations like Indonesia and Thailand – which as states are fully in control of access to their populations – the good these agencies hoped to provide would have remained purely hypothetical in nature. Ditto for well meaning international governmental agencies such as the United Nations.

Or consider World War II, a time in which the inhumane and murderous activities of the Nazis threatened to cast a dark shadow across much of the world. At that point in history, good intentions – no matter how great in supply – would not suffice to eliminate the evil and prevent the continued suffering of millions of innocent people. Only a military option existed; a strong army was needed, one with planes, tanks, guns and soldiers. The Red Cross could help in the effort, but by no means lead it. Its role was purely ancillary, as were the contributions of hundreds of other agencies. Only nation-states could save the world at that moment. Only nation-states could tax citizens and purchase equipment; only nation-states could draft men and form an army; and only nation-states could declare war and pursue victory. Everyone else, no matter how effective, how well run and how widely in operation, was simply second fiddle.

As these two examples illustrate, nation-states are the teams with the greatest potential to improve – or harm – the world. Therefore they, more than any other repository of human endeavor, hold the key to international development.

The Jewish Situation Before 1948

When Jacob and the seventy members of his family descended into Egypt due to a famine in the land of Canaan, he did so as the beloved father and grandfather of a large clan. Once there, those of whom the Passover *Haggada* describes as few in number, "were fruitful and increased abundantly, and multiplied, and grew exceedingly mighty," and thus became "a distinct nation." Thus, when Moses led the people out of Egypt, first to receive the Torah at Mount Sinai and then later to the borders of the Land of Israel, he did so as the trusted leader not of a single family but of a "cohesive community" bound by culture, religion, language, and of course the powerful historical experience of liberation.

Following Moses' death, his student Joshua took over and brought the nation into its promised land. Joshua conquered the land and the nation soon established all the requisite institutions of statehood. Over the next 1000 years, the Jewish people existed (with some interruptions) as a nation-state, possessing both the national consciousness of its liberation from Egypt and experience at Mount Sinai, as well as the sovereign state apparatus of kings, legislative bodies and an army. In 70 C.E., this millennia long national experience in the land of Israel came to an end. The mighty Romans conquered the land and exiled its people.

The tragedy of this exile was that it did not just put an end to the Jewish political sovereignty made possible by its national existence in a specified territory. It also put an end to the Jewish people's ability to operate at the highest level of international relations. The Jewish community went from being a major league baseball club to a minor league team.

3 WHY LAND MATTERS

The possession of land is the single most important aspect of being a nation-state. With it, everything becomes possible. Without it, many of the nation's goals will be impossible to realize. Take a look at the Book of Genesis, Chapter 12, verses 1-3:

> 1) Now the Lord said to Abram: 'Get thee out of thy country, and from thy kindred, and from thy father's home, and go to a land that I will show you. 2) And I will make of thee a great nation, and I will bless thee and make thy name great; and you will be a blessing. 3) And I will bless them that bless thee, and him that curses thee will I curse; and through you shall all the families of the earth be blessed.

The third verse – "through you shall all the families of the earth be blessed" – is arguably one of the most important verses in the entire Bible. After all, contained within it is one of the pillars of Judaism – the commandment to bring blessings to the entire world through our behavior. But we must consider the previous two verses as well, and in order.

What precedes verse three, the commandment to bring blessings to the entire world? "And I will make of thee (Abraham) a great nation." The logic of this order is undeniable. Before Abraham's descendants can bring blessings to the whole world – blessings that will reach "every family of the earth"– Abraham must first become a nation. Only as a nation, insists the text, will Abraham succeed in fulfilling this daunting task.

And next, before verse two can become operable, before Abraham can become a nation that matters (ie, with a political state), verse one must be fulfilled. "Go to the land that I will show you," reads the text. Before Abraham can become an effective nation – the prerequisite to bring blessings to the whole world – he must first go to a specific land; only through this process will he be able to actualize the subsequent promises.

Historically, when a people is exiled from its land, it not only loses its territory but also – eventually – all of the other qualities of statehood as well. Once dispersed amongst other states, the people no longer find themselves bound by a set of traditional laws and customs; to the contrary, their individual success and communal acceptance are dependent on observing and demonstrating allegiance to their new land. Self-government is replaced with foreign citizenship, and a once-distinct people maintain only a tenuous cultural allegiance to its old ways. They celebrate or commemorate a day here and there in remembrance of a proud but distant past. But that pales in comparison to the new commitment to, and pervasive influence of, the host country's laws and obligations.

Ultimately, the population itself becomes threatened. For starters, the cause of the exile itself – often war, pestilence, famine, etc, has a decimating effect on the population. Then, as absorption in a new land begins, people committed to the old nation die off and are replaced with people more interested in assimilating into the host culture than fighting a losing battle to preserve the ancient one. Assimilation, intermarriage, and simple apathy conspire to transform a once distinct national population into a non-recognizable segment of the larger majority population. Thus, nations exiled from their lands disappear from the world stage.

Unique among the nations, the case of the Jewish people is different. Exile from its land did not spell destruction of its organizational life. The Jewish people continued to pursue a vision of perfecting the world. And it should be noted with pride, given the poverty and oppression under which most Jews lived, that we conducted these affairs with a surprisingly high success rate. Unlike many other ancient peoples, Jews continued to maintain and establish unique, effective and purpose-driven communities. Wherever we wandered, we maintained our deep-rooted connections to one another, our traditions, and our vision of a better world.

Jewish law continued to bind the individual Jew to a certain way of life, and in so doing, also tied fellow Jews to each other. It enabled a relatively cohesive community and inspired an organized setting of national priorities.

And where Jewish law failed, anti-Semitism succeeded. Thus, even during those times of exile when the Jewish people did not choose to attend separate schools, maintain separate communal institutions or live in separate places, their enemies forced them to. Consequently, Jews never lost many of the most important factors inspiring self-government; a powerful sense of identity and an ability to speak (though not necessarily be heard) with a unified voice to outsiders.

So, even without the benefit of statehood we did not lose our status as a nation altogether. We relied on one another, we were inspired by those who came before us and the Divine commandments that guide us, and we remained a nation that did not disappear.

However, whatever contributions we had to offer to the world were offered from a fundamentally flawed position when compared to the status of a nation-state. Just as an individual cannot accomplish as much as a community, a nation cannot accomplish as much as a nation with a state (think the Cherokee Nation, the Kurds, the Gypsies, the Aborigine, and so on). Thus, as impressive as its contributions have been over the past 2000 years, the Jewish people's offerings to the world have been limited, in many ways similar to the deficiencies of the Red Cross or the United Nations. More often than not, Jews have had to *react* to the events of the world rather than *initiate* or direct them. Rather than pursuing their vision unhindered, Jews have been dependent upon the power, priorities and agenda of others – usually their host nations – to effect change. What's more, Jews have been influenced by these nations as much as they have tried to influence them, sometimes for good but just as often for bad. And thus, even when the Jewish people were able to effectively pursue an agenda, it was often one not fully Jewish in nature but rather an amalgam of many interests. In short, the Jewish people have not controlled their own destiny. And thus, they have not been able to maximally improve the destiny of others either.

    The world of nation-states is an elite club, and membership in this club has benefits –

including the ability to lead the world towards redemption. Our maintenance of virtual Jewish statehood was nothing short of miraculous. But lacking a sovereign state of its own for the past 2,000 years, the Jewish nation has been removed from the fully functioning nations of the world, and consequently has been denied membership in this club.

While the Jewish people maintained such qualities as population and a form of self-government, it did not possess a land, the final requirement of statehood, and thus was unable to bring about change or betterment to the world, which is exactly what the Jewish Nation aspires to.

Benefits Of Land

The Jewish Nation's return to the Land of Israel this past century thus marked an incredibly significant turning point in Jewish history. Most significantly, the acquisition of land made possible the establishment of the state – thus removing the Jewish nation from its 2000 year status of virtual statehood and returning it to the elite club of nation-states. It opens up many new avenues to fulfill certain spiritual values that only a state can pursue - values such as justice, peace, and welfare. Consider, for a moment, Judaism's passion for justice – "Justice, justice shall you pursue." In a Diaspora community, justice is a more personal matter; after all, the laws that fundamentally govern one's relations with another are guided by the host nation and not by the Jewish community itself. Should a person be placed in prison? Should he be put to death? What compensation should a victim receive? What safeguards need to be implemented to protect the innocent? Judaism has something to say on all these questions, but if none of its ideas ever enters an actual law book of the governing body, and if none of the ideas are faithfully applied by an actual law enforcement officer and promoted by an actual judicial system, then the innocent – real live, breathing people – will suffer and the guilty – genuinely cruel and evil, pain-causing people – may go free.

Almost all spiritual values can only enter the world through a physical reality. On a national level, that reality requires land. A land under sovereign control which can actualize spiritual concerns, a physical territory upon which a nation can build its unique infrastructure, erect its ideal society, and pursue its most important national dreams. For the past 2,000 years, such matters have been studied extensively in Talmudic academies and debated endlessly by the community. But they have seldom been applied – because only a sovereign state can do so.

Closeness Matters

The proximity of people, enabled by land, not only inspires *different motivations* – it creates *different results.*

A nation whose members are mostly located in one place will be stronger than a nation whose members are physically dispersed throughout the world. The former will be better able to articulate its core mission, be more successful in promoting it, and will reach a wider audience in executing it. As a consequence, such a nation will be far better equipped to transform its spiritual vision into a practical reality capable of benefiting the entire world.

For example, let us assume that the various Jewish communities of the United States and the various Jewish communities of Israel would like to accomplish a certain task that requires the participation of 100,000 Jews. Both of these places have approximately the same overall Jewish population from which to draw volunteers, yet there is no doubt that the Israeli community has a great advantage in terms of ease of recruitment. After all, the American community, even before it can convince the volunteers to participate, must first find them. It must scour the phone book looking for Jewish names and create lists of potential participants. It must devise the means to reach these people, such as mailing letters or showing up at synagogues and community centers. In contrast, Israel knows exactly where the 100,000 potential volunteers are – everywhere! If someone wanted to, he could knock on the first 100,000 doors in a certain city and be done with it; he would speak with a Jew on almost every visit.

The value of a centralized location for Jews is not just that there are fewer transactional costs involved in pooling resources. There is also a greater sense of connectedness among different members of the nation that develops when its members live in close proximity, which in turn often inspires a greater desire to commit one's resources to communal benefit.

Consider the following. One of the motivating factors for investing in the national effort is a sense of obligation one feels for others within that nation. Many soldiers, for example, will tell you that they risk their lives in battle more often than not out of a sense of responsibility to their fellow soldier rather than a commitment to the cause itself. Certainly, this motivation has been a defining characteristic of the Jewish people throughout our history, from the hundreds of thousands of American Jews who marched for the freedom of Soviet Jews in the 1970's to the young college student who passes out flyers on campus defending Israel and other social justice causes today. However, no matter how great the sense of kindred spirit that exists between Jews on opposite ends of the globe may be, it cannot match the intensity of such a union that also enjoys the benefit of close proximity. For example, consider the fact that I have written much of this present work in a café in which a number of people were murdered by a suicide bomber a couple of years ago. Can someone living overseas honestly tell me that he feels closer to the waitress who survived that attack than someone who sees her on a daily basis? And if he cannot, will he be as prepared to offer resources – and know where those resources need to be invested – to help her when necessary?

Another reason why a nation located in the same physical space is stronger than a nation scattered throughout the world is due to the benefits of an increased amount of face time. Even in a world of instant global interfacing, personal face-to-face contact always provides the most meaningful way to connect with others and share ideas. The personal, human touch matters. It allows for a cross-fertilization of ideas not possible – and not as intense – amongst people separated by long distances.

So in acquiring land, the Jewish Nation also acquired a central gathering place, where all the energies, genius and skills of the entire people could mix together and be concentrated. With these attributes working in unison rather than operating as independent actors dispersed the world over, the potential for the Jewish Nation has grown dramatically. Its creations can be stronger, its values more powerful, and its ideas clearer.

Mark Twain, commenting on the possibility of a Jewish state being formed in its ancient homeland, expressed a similar sentiment as we have just noted, albeit in his uniquely witty way:

> I am not the Sultan, and I am not objecting. But if that

concentration of the cunningest brains in the world are going to be made into a free country, I think it would be politic to stop it. It will not be well to let that race find out its strength. If the horses knew theirs, we should not ride anymore.

Land Makes The Jewish People Physically Stronger

A nation without land is like a homeless person. Homelessness is an inherently weak and unstable situation. With land, we become owners of our home, our country of residence is *ours*, and we invest in it as such. Jews outside of Israel know deep down that ultimately they are guests living in someone else's home. That at the end of the day, they are merely tenants who are renting. And it is not likely that they will invest their efforts and resources *in the same way, and to the same degree,* in building and improving, say, America or France, that they would if they lived in Israel. In Israel, the Jew is the owner.

Furthermore, whereas a community of renters must 'reinvent the wheel' in every new home he moves to, a community of owners is able to build on the successes and contributions of previous generations. Over the years, the wandering nature of the Jewish people has left a trail of unconnected contributions to a variety of civilizations. Jews built thriving institutions in Babylonia – colleges and hospitals and social organizations – only to be dispersed and have to start all over in a new place. The story then repeated itself in England and France, where Jews were again expelled, then in Spain (expelled in 1492)…and again and again. Rather than building on the physical accomplishments of their ancestors, Jews have had to expend valuable and limited resources recreating them. Rather than adding a new wing to an existing hospital, Jews have had to build new hospitals from scratch over and over, and thus that new wing, and more advanced care, never materialized.

In our own land, we can keep building on the shoulders of those that came before us, building a stronger and powerful society.

4 ANCIENT ISRAEL

Ancient Israel's Contributions To Modern Society

If you want to really understand the potential of a Jewish state to change the world you need only look at ancient Israel. After all, 3000 years ago there *was* a Jewish state that fulfilled this role. And that state lasted almost 1,000 years. During its existence, it possessed all those qualities necessary to constitute a true nation – a territory, a population, and a government. It also possessed the ability to utterly transform the world. And it did just that. The first Jewish state created a reality that made Western civilization possible. As Samuel Adams once quipped, "We owe more to the Jews than to any other civilization."

To this very day, the values of this state and the political ideas it first introduced to the world as a state – concepts such as *liberty, equality, justice, progress, peace, and human dignity* – continue to animate and influence all of the Western world. Today, of course, such values are a given for any civilized society, so obviously good and inherently true that one must wonder how a world could possibly have existed without them. But it did – and for a long time. That we view them today as self-evident is proof of just how powerful they really are, how fully integrated they are into our collective consciousness.

Perhaps even more spectacular than the concepts themselves that ancient Israel introduced to the world is the way it did so. This ancient Jewish state came to exert such influence not by way of war, by conquering land and imposing its principles on powerless invaded populations, as was the way of the Romans, Greeks, Syrians, Egyptians, and subsequent dominant world cultures such as Christianity (under the leadership of the Holy Roman Empire) and Islam (under the early Jihadists). No, the dominance of the values of the ancient Jewish state was achieved not through force, but rather by spirit. Its ideals and laws were recorded in the Bible, and have thus been available ever since – void of coercion, absent of imposition – to whoever has sought out their inspiration.

Furthermore, when Israel first offered its values to the world, few people – and even fewer nations – sought such inspiration. To the contrary, not only did they not adopt these principles, they attempted to uproot them from the heritage of common humanity. To the populations of the ancient world, much of what emanated from the Jewish state stood in stark contrast to their own entrenched value systems.

Liberty

Egyptian society, for example, was built – quite literally – on the backs of slaves. For that matter, so too was almost every other ancient society. Indeed, it would not be an exaggeration to assert that the vast majority of all peoples during that time were born, lived and died in slavery, never once breathing freedom's air. *Israel's emphasis on liberty – "Proclaim thee liberty throughout the land" – and abhorrence of lording over another was a revolutionary call to dismantle the very essence of these cultures.*

Equality

In Babylonia Hammurabi's code enshrined a society which favored the wealthy and powerful as a matter of law at the expense of the poor and lowly. *In stark contrast, the Jewish nation introduced the value of equality before the law, clearly encapsulated in its own Biblical code: "Don't favor the wealthy or poor."* Even kings were not to be treated with preferred status.

For that matter, all three branches of the leadership of ancient Israel – the king, the priests, and the prophets – had limitations placed on their powers to safeguard against corruption and abuse of power. In many ways, then, the governance of ancient Israel was the forerunner – and inspiration – of today's irreplaceable system of checks and balances that exists in any legitimate form of government.

Peace

The Roman Empire was based on the premise of uniting the world through force. It arrogantly called its Empire the Pax Romana, the

Peace of Rome, as if to say peace was simply the lack of rebellion from the subjects brutally subdued following their conquest. The Romans, of course, were not alone in elevating the value of war and world domination. The warrior is also the ideal among Brahmins, Homeric, Hellenes, Celts and Vikings." *In contrast, Israel's hero was the pursuer of peace.* Its vision of national success had nothing to do with world domination. As the Prophet declared, the ideal sought by Jewish 'power' was a world in which nations "shall beat their swords into plowshares, and their spears into pruning hooks; nation shall not lift up sword against nation, neither shall they learn war any more" Such a vision was detested by the surrounding peoples. For them, the pursuer of peace was a weakling, the cause of distress, not the source of pride.

Human Dignity

The Greeks, meanwhile, believed in beauty as an absolute value, which in turn enabled them to go to war – and force the deaths of hundreds of thousands – simply over the beauty of a woman (as with Helen of Troy). It also inspired them to abandon at birth deformed children. *The Jewish state, however, transformed its religious belief that every human being is created in the Image of God into the political right that every person must be protected by the state, regardless of physical, mental or intellectual status.*

Progress and Free Will

And then, of course, there were all the cultic religions that worshipped nature above all else. In such systems, human endeavor was irrelevant; after all, nature predetermined the outcome of all efforts, and thus it was futile to attempt anything except learning to accept the world as it was. Nothing could be done about the suffering of the weak or the corruption of the powerful. *In contrast, Judaism – and its political arm, the first state of Israel – elevated free moral will and human endeavor as a means to perfect the world.* Nature might have set the ground rules, but it was very much in humanity's power to alter the situation, to alleviate suffering and to uproot the corruption. That the Jewish state believed the world could improve, that history could progress, established it as a revolutionary force, one concerned with overturning the status quo.

Numerous other examples of ancient societies opposed to the ideas and values introduced by the Jewish State abound. What connects them all is their belief – which of course was accurate – that these new principles threatened the privileged status enjoyed by the major powers of the time.

In time, though, many of these ideas so vehemently rejected began to infiltrate and take root. Then, even more amazingly, these values began to transform these powers from within, eventually becoming the very foundations from which these powers spread *their* influence throughout the world.

While the acceptance of these values began in small doses during the existence of the ancient Jewish state itself, and then slowly proceeded with the early growth of other religions and political philosophies that adopted them as their own, the true impact of these ideas did not become readily apparent until the last few hundred years. During this time, these fundamental ideas have become the seminal values upon which all decent modern societies have based their existence.

As Thomas Cahill, the author of *The Gift of the Jews,* adds:

> *For better or worse, the role of the West in humanity's*

> *history is singular. Because of this, the role of the Jews, the inventors of Western culture, is also singular; there is simply no one else remotely like them.*

America and Western Civilization

Perhaps the best way to appreciate the contribution of ancient Israel to the world is by taking a tour of some of the leading civilized nations of the Western world. For it is these societies that are the greatest recipients of the aforementioned ideas. As U.S. President Woodrow Wilson once noted, "the laws of Moses … constitute the gross substance of our present habit, both as regards the sphere of private life, and as regards action of the state."

Therefore, it is also these societies – at least when they gave voice to these millennia-old values – that are the intellectual and spiritual heirs of ancient Israel. In many respects, then, their contributions to civilization – East and West – also attest to the true nature of ancient Israel's impact on the world.

A quite logical place to begin is with the early stirrings of liberal national awakening in European lands. As Joseph Jacobs noted in 1919, "the book that made the Jews has also, in large measure, laid the foundation of European civilization. In all matters spiritual, the Bible is the one common fountain-head of European thought and feeling."

To appreciate just how accurate these words are, let us narrow our tour to 17th century England. The preference for constitutional governance in much of modern Europe (and much of the subsequent democratic world) draws its inspiration from this time and place. And it, in turn, drew its inspiration from the Bible and ancient Israel. Indeed, one of the specific aims of the revolt at that time was the establishment of a Monarchy similar to the Jewish state – yes, kings should exist and have power, but their power must be limited by the law and traditions. Consider but one extremely simple, but undeniably powerful example of the link between the British push for good governance and the inspiration provided by ancient Israel: The

English rebellion – which ushered in an age of checks and balances, the concern for individual rights, and an emphasis on personal liberty began with the cry: "To your tents, O' Israel."

Shortly thereafter, across the English Channel, the French middle class stormed the Bastille in the attempt to rid the nation of an unrestrained and tyrannical monarch. Their battle cry did not mention Israel by name, but it did include the specific values it introduced to the world – against the tide – a few thousand years earlier: Liberty, Equality and Brotherhood. The French Revolution, in turn, provided the inspiration and intellectual fortitude for many a subsequent European liberation movement.

Now let us travel across the Atlantic and begin exploring the shores of the new world. In Boston, we will find the Old South Meeting Hall, the site where men like John Hancock and Samuel Adams inspired the crowd with fiery oration to throw off the yoke of the British king just as the ancient Jews achieved freedom from Pharaoh. Just a short distance away, in New Haven, on the crest of Yale University, are the very words that adorned the breast plate of the High Priest of ancient Israel – *Light and Truth* – in Hebrew no less! In fact, the founders of Yale were so enamored with the Jewish state, they insisted that Hebrew be a required course so that students could study the Bible in the original. The Valedictorian speeches in the early years –

and the President's address at graduation – were actually given in Hebrew. Our next stop: New York City and the United Nations – the great hope (unfortunately often unrealized) for a world characterized by world peace. Just outside its hallowed halls stands a wall in honor of the great Biblical prophet Isaiah; its inscription includes his powerful prayer for peace mentioned earlier: "They shall beat their swords into plowshares." In Philadelphia, the city of brotherly love, the Torah's cry "Proclaim thee liberty throughout the land" appears on the Liberty Bell.

Our final stop is Washington, DC. Here, let us not only consider the outside edifices of many buildings adorned with Biblical phrases and the exhortations of the Jewish prophets – from the

Supreme Court building to Congressional offices.

Clearly, the beliefs rooted in the original ideas of ancient Israel influenced the founders of the United States and many others, and by extension, influenced how these nations developed. What America is today – which, with warts and all, is still amongst the most free, open and successful societies in the world – was made possible by, and is based on, the existence of the first Jewish state.

Before ending our tour, let us enter the National Archives building, in which the Declaration of Independence is meticulously guarded. Perhaps more than any other document, this Declaration encapsulates the fundamental values, ideals and aspirations of American society. And here we find that it too is based on the ancient ideas of the first Jewish state.

Consider, for example, the most powerful and salient component of the Declaration of Independence: "We hold these truths to be self-evident: That all men are created equal; that they are endowed by their Creator with certain unalienable rights; that among these are life, liberty and the pursuit of happiness; and that to secure these rights, governments are instituted by men." All these assertions were introduced to the world by the ancient Jewish state.

What our brief tour demonstrates is that the innovations of the ancient Jewish state are the most fundamental values of the United States and the other Western nations. To the extent that the

United States promotes these values represents a continuing contribution of the first Jewish state.

Two thousand years ago we had a state. That state revolutionized the foundations of world culture. It shifted reality on a *philosophical level* by altering the value systems upon which all of humanity rested. But then Judaism's work was abruptly truncated with the conquest and dispersion of the Jewish people.

The next step, to demonstrate how to actuate those values on a *practical basis,* was cut short. Judaism's work, the Jewish people being a light unto the nations, was left unfinished. Until now. Today we are back in the amazing position where, if we want to, we can build the nation of Israel according to the values, our values, that inspired the world. This is something that no nation has ever done.

Exporting Ideas

Ideas have always been the greatest export of the Jewish people. In fact, Rabbi Abraham Kook argues that the production of ideas – and the vision, prophecy and truth that accompany them – is the essential characteristic of life in the land of Israel. He suggests that every nation has a special contribution to make to the world, and that every land upon which a nation exists has a special quality. A natural resource if you will. Saudi Arabia, for example, has oil. South Africa has gold and diamonds. America has timber, not to mention a whole array of other resources. Israel's natural resource is ideas.

Thankfully, the ideas our ancestors offered to the world were good. Not just good – logical and well-reasoned – but *good* – morally positive and inspiring. And they have not just stood the test of time; they have transformed the world. The world is a different and better place because of ancient Israel's contributions. They provided the foundation for entire societies and encouraged them to become the best they can be. They gave hope to the prisoner wrongly accused and guidance to authors of constitutions. They liberated oppressed people and gave strength to those fighting against evil worldwide. They made the lives of average people better, and improved the moral compass of all of humanity.

Can you imagine the world today if the values of ancient Rome – the values of the Coliseum, the Gladiator – had persevered instead?

5 THE STATE OF ISRAEL

The re-birth of a sovereign Jewish nation-state is the single most significant achievement of the twentieth century. *The return to our land, is a return to relevance, a process that returns the Jewish people to the highest level of international influence.* After all, more than anything else, the creation of a Jewish nation-state has brought the *ability* of the Jewish people to perfect the world up to par with its *aspirations* and vision of perfecting the world. The dissonance between desire and capability that has hampered the Jewish people throughout its 2,000 year exile has thus been removed.

And just how will this Israel change the world? Through the power of modeling. Understanding the power of modeling is fundamental in order to appreciate how the Jewish people will eventually provide their most significant contribution to the betterment of the world.

It is important to note that to serve as a model for others, the 'others' have to actually see you. So too with the Jewish people. When an individual Jew engages in positive behavior, it is possible that another individual – Jew or non-Jew – might be inspired and do the same. When a Jewish community builds a hospital, another community – again Jewish or non-Jewish – might be inspired and duplicate the actions of the first.

A nation, however, is unlikely to draw inspiration from either. An individual and a local community are entirely different entities than a nation, lacking both compelling relevance for, and a powerful influence on, the latter. A nation will generally only model its behavior on something it can relate to directly – and that is another nation.

This is the crux of the matter. For the past 2,000 years, the nations of the world have not viewed the Jewish people as one of the gang. We might have considered ourselves a nation – and indeed we were on some level – but *they* didn't. And thus it is hard to be a 'light unto the nations' without first being recognized as a nation oneself.

This is why returning to the Land of Israel has been such an essential a step for the People of

Israel. In reacquiring our land, we have also reacquired statehood; and in reacquiring statehood, we have reacquired normalcy and influence. Now, unlike our wandering existence for the past 2,000 years, the nations of the world can once again draw inspiration from our actions in the most concrete of ways. Now, when the Jewish Nation – a nation-state like all others – models what is right, what priorities must be established, and how such objectives can be accomplished, the 'people' watching are not individuals, not communities, but other nations as well. And watch they do. *Consider, for example, that there are more international journalists in Israel per capita than any other place in the world.* The eyes of the world quite literally watch whatever takes place here. Thus, after an unbearably long 2,000 year absence, the Jewish nation has once again been elevated to the highest level of international relevance. In so doing, it can once again leverage a concern for a specific cause into an international concern – and as we noted previously, it is on this level of concern, and only this level of concern, that the potential exists to touch every person on the planet.

6 IMAGINE

How might this work? Consider, as an example, the problem of world poverty. Solving this matter is obviously of great concern to all people of good will throughout the world. Unfortunately, as previously noted, individuals can only have a limited impact in eliminating this problem. So too is this the case with international aid agencies, partly because of limited budgets and partly because of obstructionist governments preventing them from reaching those in greatest need.

Nations – the entities that could make the greatest impact – have by and large sat out this great fight. The United States, for example, is the most generous of all nations when it comes to international aid. And yet, all it gives to humanitarian causes outside its borders is less than one-half of one percent of its national budget. The contributions of other nations are abysmal.

Now imagine the representative of the nation of Israel rising in the chambers of the United Nations. Listen to him say something amazing: "Although we are a small nation, and despite the fact that our resources are smaller than many other nations, we have decided to try to tackle the problem of world poverty. Henceforth, we will give 10% of our national budget to humanitarian causes outside of our borders. We believe this is what God would want. This is what we believe will help eliminate tremendous suffering, and fulfill God's vision of treating every human with dignity and respect."

What would the response of the other nations be?

If only the ten wealthiest nations increased their contributions to just 5% of their budget, they would produce *seven times the amount of money necessary to eliminate world hunger!* With such a change of international priorities, it might then become possible to consider the potential elimination of many ills that were once thought to be unsolvable problems. How many people's lives will be saved? How many more millions will see their lives dramatically improved?

Now imagine if, rather than a nation making the above statement, an individual did so. Would *nations* be inspired to respond in kind? Would the reach be nearly as great? Of course not. An individual might *do* the exact same things a nation might do, but an individual cannot *achieve* the same results via the same action. An individual who gives 10% of his funds away would never be able to match the collective power of the wealthiest nations.

Now imagine what might happen if the next month, the Israeli representative rises once again and declares that Israel is implementing by far the most stringent environmental laws on the planet. The country will generate 100% of its electricity from solar energy, 100% of its water from ocean desalination, and 100% of its new cars sold will be totally electric, within eighteen years.

And what happens if a few months later he rises again? By now, the other representatives are leery of what might come next. How much is he going to cost me this time? Deep inside, though, they admire him. He and his nation are changing the world. He is doing something no one thought possible, but of course is quite possible. This time, when the representative stands to speak, he says Israel will no longer stand idly by in the face of the Biblical prohibition of *Tzar Ba'aley Chaim*, the exploitation and suffering imposed on animals. It will require far higher standards than exist anywhere in the world to protect and provide for the quality of life for all animals. Factory farming practiced by the food industry the world over, will come to an end in Israel. This means that the cost of eating animals will increase, but Israelis will compensate with a more plant-based diet. Animals will have rights and will no longer be cruelly treated as commodities.

These regular announcements – and accompanying behavior – would be relentless. Sometimes, they would have little effect. Other times, though, they would inspire nations to respond in kind. And when a nation responds, it's of an entirely different quality than when an individual, or even a voluntary community, responds. A nation would pass laws requiring certain behavior, and these laws would reach – by definition – every single person within its boundaries. One announcement in the United Nations, then, could have a greater impact than a lifetime of work in the field. One speech could have the ripple effect of influencing 170 nations, which in turn could influence 6 billion people.

The world is a large place. Reaching its entire population with an idea is consequently a monumental task. Doing so via the mechanism of a nation – and the relations that nation has with other nations – is the best way to overcome the challenge.

Now we can now enter the big leagues. Now we are a nation with a land, a government, a preeminent army, world class health care, transportation, and education systems – you name it, we have everything like anywhere else. Now, we are a nation like any other nation. And more importantly, now we can become a nation unlike any other nation.

7 THE ZIONIST

Zionism does not exist to make us free to do whatever we want to do – free *from* others – but rather, it is exists to make us free to serve others, to be a light unto the nations. When the nation within us is silent – either because there is no state, as was the case for the past 2,000 years, or because a nation exists but it lacks vision and the right behavior – then the Jewish people remain enslaved. When the nation is permitted to sing its song, then we are truly liberated to fulfill our ultimate purpose.

Yesterday, Jews came to Israel in large numbers to escape persecution or economic hardship. Today, Israel's economic standard of living is about to eclipse that of Europe, and is expected to surpass even the United States within the next few decades. Although many American Jews have not yet realized it, they no longer need to decide between living in Israel and economic prosperity.

Today Zionism is approaching a tipping point. The nation has been reconstituted. The next step, though, remains unrealized. That is the step of infusing the national consciousness with its historic meaning and direction, which in turn will shine its beauty outwards illuminating the entire world. I have written this book to be a small part of that process.

I am incredibly optimistic about the new Jewish state. If one wants to understand just how great an impact our new modern Jewish state can have, consider the result the last time the people of Israel got together and created a state. Look what we did as a small nation of former slaves so many years ago. Look what we accomplished, and look how much of an impact those accomplishments continue to make.

What will the innovations of this new Jewish state look like? I'm not sure. But gathering the most disproportionately talented group of people the world has ever known – the Jews – together in one spot spells both spiritual and economic superpower, if history is any guide. Torah scholars, scientists, engineers, entrepreneurs, Nobel prize laureates from every field – the Israel our children will gaze upon will be *the* place to be. To be a participant in making it happen, and being able to give it to them, well, that's your call…

ABOUT THE AUTHOR

Ian Pear is the founder and Rabbi of Shir Hadash, a well known Synagogue and Educational Institute in Jerusalem. Prior to establishing Shir Hadash, he was the director of the Hillel Foundation at Tel Aviv University, home to the largest Jewish student population in the world.

He received his ordination from Yeshiva University, a law degree from New York University, and a degree in international law from Georgetown University.

Made in the USA
Charleston, SC
02 March 2012